Pebble™

DATE DUE

JUN 2 2 2013		

DEMCO 38-296

Pebble Books are published by Capstone Press,
1710 Roe Crest Drive, North Mankato, Minnesota 56003
www.capstonepub.com

Library of Congress Cataloging-in-Publication Data
Carlson, Cheryl.
    Dr. Seuss / by Cheryl Carlson
    p. cm.—(First biographies)
    Includes bibliographical references and index.
    ISBN-13: 978-0-7368-3639-5 (hardcover)   ISBN-10: 0-7368-3639-X (hardcover)
    ISBN-13: 978-0-7368-5091-9 (softcover)   ISBN-10: 0-7368-5091-0 (softcover)
    1. Seuss, Dr.—Juvenile literature. 2. Authors, American—20th century—
Biography—Juvenile literature. 3. Illustrators—United States—Biography—Juvenile
literature. 4. Children's literature—Authorship—Juvenile literature. I. Title. II. First
biographies (Mankato, Minn.)
PS3513.E2Z623 2005
813'.52—dc22   2004011904
Summary: Simple text and photographs present the life of Dr. Seuss.

Note to Parents and Teachers

The First Biographies set supports national history standards
for units on people and culture. This book describes and illustrates
the life of Dr. Seuss. The images support early readers in
understanding the text. The repetition of words and phrases helps
early readers learn new words. This book also introduces early
readers to subject-specific vocabulary words, which are defined in
the Glossary section. Early readers may need assistance to read
some words and to use the Table of Contents, Glossary, Read More,
Internet Sites, and Index sections of the book.

Table of Contents

Time Line

1904
born

Early Years

Dr. Seuss was born in 1904 in Massachusetts. His real name was Theodor Seuss Geisel.

◄ childhood home in Springfield, Massachusetts

Time Line

1904
born

1920
graduates from
high school

As a child, Dr. Seuss liked to read. He graduated from high school in 1920. He worked on a magazine. Then he went to college in England.

Springfield High School; yearbook picture of Dr. Seuss (inset)

Time Line

1904	1920	1937
born	graduates from	writes first book
	high school	

Writing and Drawing

After college, Dr. Seuss made money drawing. He had his own studio. Dr. Seuss wrote and illustrated his first book in 1937.

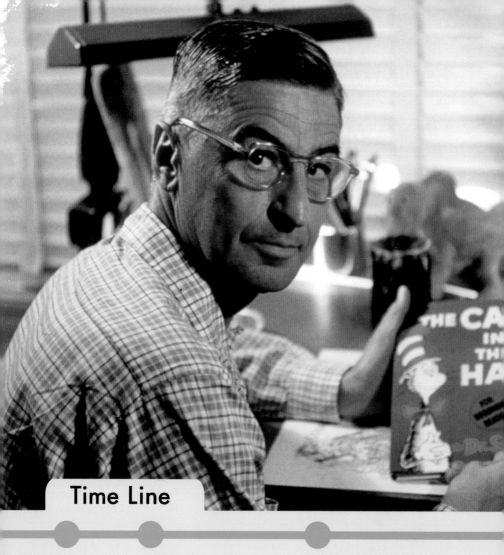

Time Line

1904
born

1920
graduates from
high school

1937
writes first book

In 1957, Dr. Seuss wrote *The Cat in the Hat.* The book used rhymes to tell the story of a silly cat. Dr. Seuss drew funny pictures for the book.

1957
writes *The Cat in the Hat*

Time Line

1904
born

1920
graduates from
high school

1937
writes first book

Many children loved the stories and drawings by Dr. Seuss. Some of his books were made into movies.

1957
writes *The Cat in the Hat*

Time Line

1904	1920	1937
born	graduates from high school	writes first book

Adults also liked stories
and drawings by Dr. Seuss.
He won many awards
for his books and movies.

Dr. Seuss (center) holds one of his awards

1957
writes *The Cat in the Hat*

Time Line

1904
born

1920
graduates from
high school

1937
writes first book

Dr. Seuss wrote and illustrated 44 books during his lifetime. He died in 1991.

1957
writes *The Cat in the Hat*

1991
dies

Time Line

1904	1920	1937
born	graduates from high school	writes first book

Remembering Dr. Seuss

A library in California is named after Dr. Seuss. People can see a statue of him at the library.

1957
writes *The Cat in the Hat*

1991
dies

Time Line

1904
born

1920
graduates from
high school

1937
writes first book

In 2004, a Hollywood Star was named for Dr. Seuss. Today, people still read and love books that Dr. Seuss wrote.

1957
writes *The Cat in the Hat*

1991
dies

2004
receives Hollywood Star

Glossary

award—a prize; Dr. Seuss won a Peabody Award, a Pulitzer Prize, an Academy Award, and many others.

college—a place where people study after high school

illustrate—to draw pictures for books

library—a place where books, magazines, newspapers, and other materials are kept for reading and borrowing

rhyme—words that end with the same sound; poems and stories sometimes use rhyme.

studio—a room or building where an artist works

Read More

Adil, Janeen R. *Dr. Seuss.* A Robbie Reader. Hockessin, Del.: Mitchell Lane, 2004.

Lynch, Wendy. *Dr. Seuss.* Lives and Times. Chicago: Heinemann Library, 2000.

Rau, Dana Meachen. *Dr. Seuss.* Rookie Biography. New York: Children's Press, 2003.

Internet Sites

FactHound offers a safe, fun way to find Internet sites related to this book. All of the sites on FactHound have been researched by our staff.

Here's how:

1. Visit *www.facthound.com*

2. Type in this special code **073683639X** for age-appropriate sites. Or enter a search word related to this book for a more general search.

3. Click on the **Fetch It** button.

FactHound will fetch the best sites for you!

23

Index

Word Count: 184
Grade: 1
Early-Intervention Level: 16

Editorial Credits
Sarah L. Schuette, editor; Heather Kindseth, set designer; Patrick D. Dentinger, book designer; Kelly Garvin, photo researcher; Scott Thoms, photo editor

Photo Credits
AP/Wide World Photos, cover; Lenny Ignelzi, 18; Reed Saxon, 20
Corbis/Bettmann, 14; James L. Amos, 16
Courtesy of the Connecticut Valley Historical Museum, Springfield, Massachusetts, 4, 6 (inset)
Getty Images Inc./Gene Lester, 8, 10, 12
New York Public Library, 6 (main)
US Postal Service, 1